A SLOTH'S GUIDE
TO ETIQUETTE

A SLOTH'S GUIDE TO ETIQUETTE

A LAID-BACK APPROACH TO SOCIALLY ACCEPTABLE BEHAVIOR

Sarah Jackson

DOG 'n' BONE

Published in 2020 by Dog 'n' Bone Books
an imprint of Ryland Peters & Small Ltd
20-21 Jockey's Fields   341 E 116th St
London WC1R 4BW   New York, NY 10029

www.rylandpeters.com

10 9 8 7 6 5 4 3 2 1

A CIP catalog record for this book is available from the
Library of Congress and the British Library.

ISBN: 978 1 912983 21 6

Printed in China

Illustrator: Sarah Jackson
Designer: Eliana Holder

CONTENTS

HI. MY NAME'S BRIAN AND I'M A THREE-TOED SLOTH. I'M HERE TO TALK TO YOU ABOUT ETIQUETTE...

Perhaps you purchased this book because you know how important it is to display proper etiquette and would like a few pointers. Or maybe a concerned friend or family member has recognized that you have the manners of a pig at an all-you-can-eat buffet and has decided it's time you sorted yourself out. Whatever the case, I'm here to guide you through the minefield that is "correct etiquette" with some advice and practical pointers on how to conduct yourself with the utmost decorum.

You may be thinking "what can a three-toed sloth teach me about etiquette that I can't just find on the internet?"

Well, a different perspective... that's what.

While you humans are intent on spending all your time with your eyes glued to a screen, I've been taking all the time in the world to relax, observe life, and learn about the finer points of etiquette (in between sleeping and eating, of course). Plus, we sloths are just naturally well mannered, easy going, totally charming, good natured folk.

So trust me... I'm an expert.

WHAT EXACTLY IS "GOOD ETIQUETTE?"

According to the dictionary:

"Etiquette is the customary code of polite behavior in society or among members of a particular profession or group."

To put it simply, good etiquette is behaving yourself and poor etiquette is... well, not behaving yourself.

Sounds simple, huh? Well, let me tell you, it doesn't come as naturally to everyone as it does us sloths.

Like Tony, the common warthog...

It probably doesn't come as a surprise that common warthogs are not known for their politeness and decent table manners... and Tony is no exception.

AND IT'S NOT JUST HIS MANNERS THAT STINK!

But even a common warthog can tidy his act up and learn some manners. It may not be easy at times, but just remember: if Tony can do it, then so can you.

THE BASICS

Well, I think it's about time we get started with the basics. These are simple rules that you should apply to any situation, wherever you are, and whoever you are with. NO EXCEPTIONS. These should be fairly straightforward, so if you're struggling with them then you definitely need some help.

1. SMILE. A smile shows that you are polite, happy, and fun to be around and will instantly make you more likeable. Smiling at others has been proven to make them feel more relaxed and comfortable in your company. Go on, give it a try.

2. ALWAYS REMEMBER TO SAY PLEASE AND THANK YOU.
Whatever situation you find yourself in, maintaining good manners is vital and should never be forgotten.

HELLO!
MAY I EAT YOU...
PLEASE?

3. DON'T BE LATE. This is the hardest of all the basic principles for us sloths. Running late for meetings, whether for work or pleasure, is not acceptable. If you struggle with tardiness I suggest you put some simple measures in place to help you with your time management.

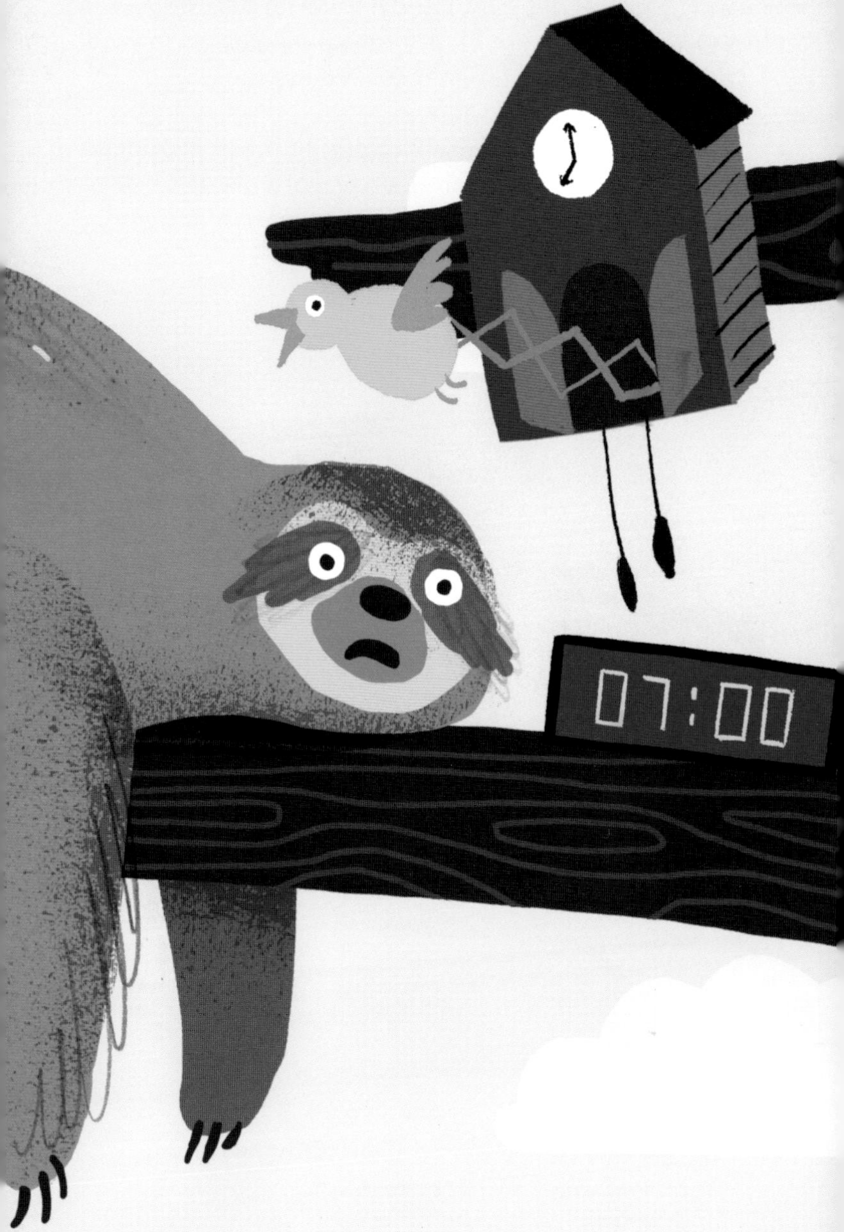
07:00

4. LOOK PEOPLE IN THE EYE WHEN YOU TALK TO THEM. It shows that you are interested in what they have to say (even if you're not).

Sometimes it's not possible, but, in these instances, just try not to focus on their private areas or any body part that they may be self conscious about.

NB: always remember to blink. Otherwise you might look a bit too intense.

5. DON'T PICK YOUR NOSE. I know it's tempting to see what tasty morsels are lurking up there, but picking your nose is the kind of thing that might get you thrown out of a dinner party. My advice: blow your nose into the nearest leaf and discreetly put it to one side for a proper inspection in private later on.

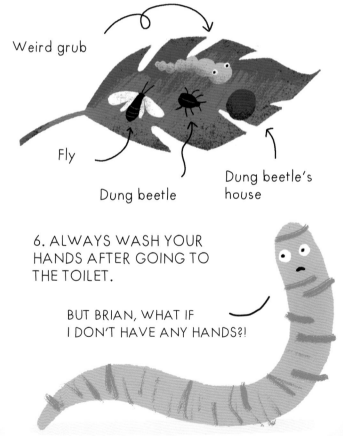

Weird grub

Fly

Dung beetle

Dung beetle's house

6. ALWAYS WASH YOUR HANDS AFTER GOING TO THE TOILET.

BUT BRIAN, WHAT IF I DON'T HAVE ANY HANDS?!

FIRST IMPRESSIONS

Now that we've dealt with the basics, it's time to look at first impressions.

This is *soooo* important. Research shows that most people take just seven seconds to determine their first impression of someone (for us sloths it takes a little bit longer), which just goes to show that you really must do your best in those first few moments of meeting.

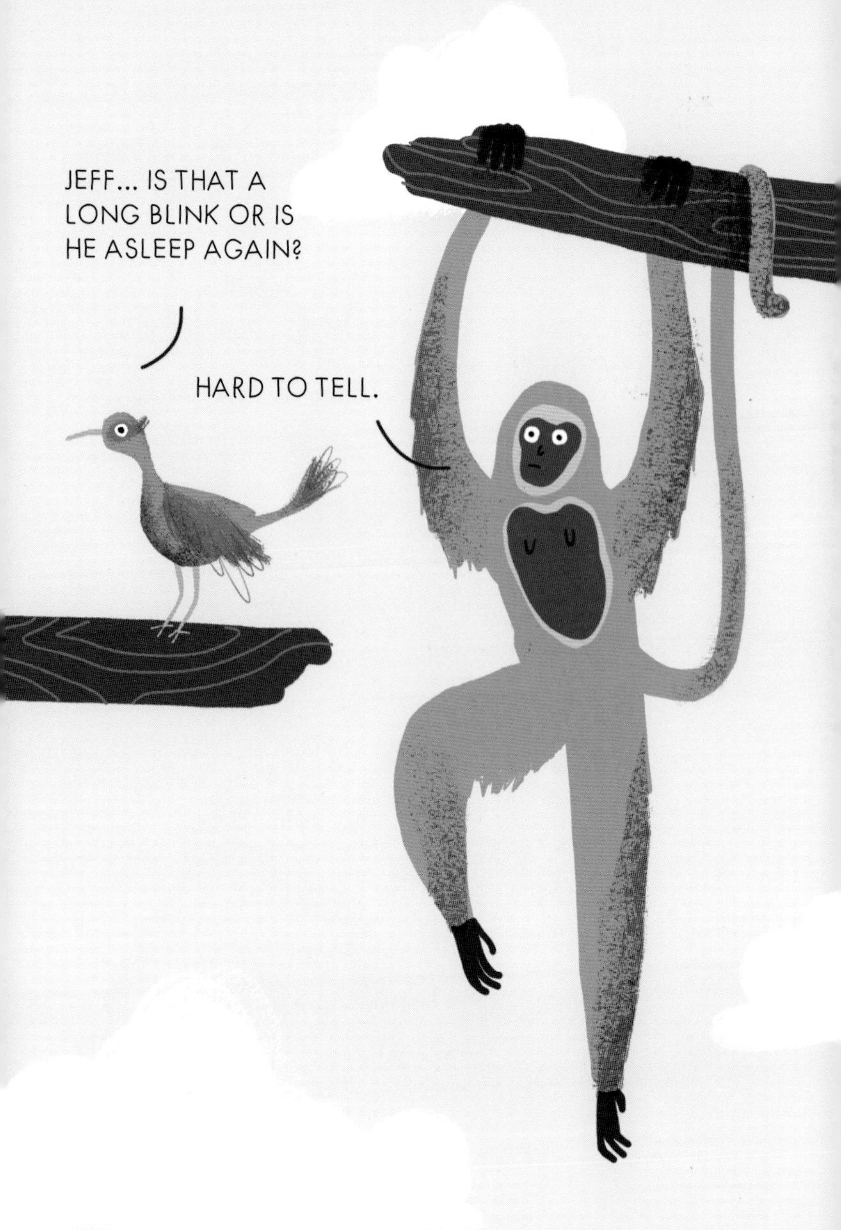
JEFF... IS THAT A LONG BLINK OR IS HE ASLEEP AGAIN?
HARD TO TELL.

PERSONAL GROOMING

Looking your best is important. It's not enough to just roll out of bed, dust the moss off your fur, and expect to look good.

To create a good impression you need to make sure your personal grooming habits are tip-top. That doesn't mean spending hours on end preening yourself with fancy products. A hot shower and a quick comb of the hair will get you off to a good start.

It's also important to smell good... you don't want bad smells to leave a lingering impression on people. If your natural body odor leaves a lot to be desired, try rubbing yourself against something that smells good, in the hope that the lovely aroma transfers to you.

NB: be discreet when rubbing against things in public places. You don't want to cause alarm.

MEETING NEW PEOPLE

When meeting new people it's important to greet them correctly. A "hello" and a polite handshake is generally considered to be good etiquette, although some folk have different ideas...

Know that not everyone's customs are the same as yours, so it's always good to approach new people with an open mind. And if you are happy to embrace new ways of greeting people, then go for it.

SNIFF, SNIFF!

It's great etiquette to pay someone a compliment when you meet them. Here are a few suggestions to get you started...

POLITE CONVERSATION

Sometimes engaging in conversation with strangers can feel intimidating, but don't be scared. Come prepared with a few discussion points to get the talk flowing. Here's a list of some of my favorite topics to get you going:

Can you ever have TOO much sleep?

What are the best times to nap?

Which is tastier, tree grubs or flies?

How to recognize a baboon butt when you're hanging upside down.

TOP TIP: keep it light. Nobody wants to get stuck talking to a fun sponge...

Fun sponge sucks the fun out of everything. Avoid at all costs.

LISTENING IS IMPORTANT

Make sure you don't dominate the conversation; it's important to let other people talk and to listen to what they have to say. But be warned... some people like to talk a LOT.

In these instances it can be very hard to pay attention (or even stay awake). It's not good etiquette to fall asleep during a conversation, so I find a couple of well-timed head nods and holding my eyes open gives the impression I'm listening, even if I'm thinking about more enjoyable things, like sleep...

(... or, in the case of a fun sponge, anything else).

DINNER PARTIES

If you're lucky enough to be invited to a dinner party then you've obviously passed the first impressions test and someone has decided they like you enough to have you as a guest (or they had a last-minute cancellation and thought you probably wouldn't have other plans). Either way, well done.

It's considered bad etiquette to turn up to a dinner party empty handed. A gift for the host, such as a bottle of something to drink, will do the job nicely. I like to bring a bottle of my home brew, but if you're not feeling creative then a stop at the nearest grocery store will do just fine.

Never bring food to a dinner party unless asked. You don't want to show up the host or imply that their cooking isn't up to scratch.

BUT WHAT IF THEIR COOKING ISN'T UP TO SCRATCH?

Good question. There's nothing worse than being served a bad meal, but it's rude to tell someone their cooking is terrible, and if you leave a full plate you might as well tell them their food tastes like a rotten witchetty grub (not good). My tip: look for the nearest plant pot and tip the contents of your plate in when nobody's looking, then declare loudly what a delicious meal it was. Trust me, everyone will be happy.*

*Except the plant.

DID YOU KNOW... ?

It's generally considered very rude to burp at the dinner table. It should be avoided at all costs. HOWEVER, my friend Jenny tells me that in certain parts of China and India it's considered a polite way of thanking the chef for a satisfying meal.

Fancy that!

BELCH!

YOU'RE VERY
WELCOME, JENNY.

NB: it's never acceptable to burp the alphabet.

ETIQUETTE IN THE WORKPLACE

It's important to maintain a professional demeanor in the workplace in order to stay in favor with your colleagues and to avoid getting fired.

When communicating with workmates be aware of certain phrases that could be construed as negative or unhelpful. Choose your words carefully to get a better response...

THAT'S AN INTERESTING CONCEPT, KEITH. LET'S ADD IT TO THE MAYBE PILE...

Maybe (not)

(... THAT'S A RUBBISH IDEA, KEITH, AND NOBODY LIKES IT.)

I'M EXPERIENCING HIGH WORKFLOW LEVELS AT THE MOMENT SO WILL BE OFFLINE UNTIL I'VE CAUGHT UP.

IT'S A CHALLENGING ENVIRONMENT IN THE OFFICE AT THE MOMENT, HOWEVER I HOPE THE ISSUES WILL BE RESOLVED SOON...

(... PETER* IN ACCOUNTS IS RUBBISH AT HIS JOB BUT I'VE HEARD HE'S GETTING LAID OFF.)

*Peter's name has been changed to protect his identity.

WEDDINGS

Weddings are often formal occasions where, as well as the usual rules of etiquette, there are some traditions and additional guidelines to follow. In fact, there are too many to cover in this book alone, so I'll just give you these three very important tips for good wedding etiquette...

1. NEVER EVER WEAR WHITE AS THIS MAY UPSTAGE THE BRIDE.

WHO INVITED PAULINE?!

2. DON'T EAT THE CAKE UNTIL IT'S BEEN CUT.

3. AND WHATEVER YOU DO, DON'T FORGET TO TELL THE BRIDE HOW LOVELY SHE LOOKS.

SOCIAL MEDIA

It's impossible to avoid being on social media nowadays (unless you're over the age of 80), and even the most remote places in the world can stay connected thanks to modern technology. But the world wide web can be a complicated place, and if you're not familiar with online etiquette you could slip up. Here are my tips for staying "social media savvy" and how to get the best from all that the online community has to offer.

HELLO? HELLO? CAN YOU HEAR ME?

I DON'T THINK IT'S
MEAT TO WORK LIKE
THIS, DARREN...

THE ONLINE COMMUNITY

Social media is great for meeting people, making friends, and mixing with folk that you wouldn't necessarily make contact with in real life. It's there to be enjoyed and can be a pleasurable way to pass the time, but before you throw yourself into it you need to be aware of certain behaviors that are frowned upon in the online community...

1. OVERUSE OF HASHTAGS. A hashtag is a way of tagging your image so that people can find it if they're looking for specific content, e.g. #SLOTH (naturally, a very popular search term!). People also like to use them to emphasize a point in sentences too, but be warned:

THE OVERUSE OF HASHTAGS WILL JUST COME ACROSS AS #ANNOYING AND WILL MAKE PEOPLE #MAD BEACUSE IT'S A LITTLE BIT #PRETENTIOUS AND PEOPLE WOULD RATHER YOU JUST #TALKNORMALLY BECAUSE WHO EVEN SEARCHES FOR ALL THESE #RANDOMWORDS ANYWAY?

2. PHOTO SPAMMING. It's great to share what you've been up to, but you need to be aware that not everyone is as interested in your life, holidays, new haircut, kid, kid's new haircut, kid's first day at school, etc., etc... sorry to break it to you.

I should also tell you that people aren't interested in seeing what you've had for breakfast or a picture of your iced frappuccino... especially if it's being drunk on the way to an early morning yoga class. Nobody likes a show off.

3. OVERSHARING. Resisit the urge to share too much on the internet for all to see. There are certain things that are best kept for friends and family only, such as daily gripes and moans about life, divisive opinions, political views, arguments with the local neighborhood busybody, and unpredictable toilet habits.

Remember this: you wouldn't air your dirty laundry in public, so don't do it on the internet.

IT WAS BROWN WHEN I BOUGHT IT!

4. TROLLING. Let's talk about internet trolls. An internet troll is a rather uncouth individual who starts quarrels with members of the online community for their own entertainment. They may deliberately try to upset someone by posting negative comments online and are nasty folk with a total disregard for others.

If you suspect someone is trolling you, don't be tempted to engage with them, you'll just be doing what they want.

Internet trolls rarely look like actual trolls. In fact, most real trolls don't even have the internet because they live under bridges.

I JUST CAN'T GET WIFI DOWN HERE...

ROMANCE

Oh what a minefield dating is in today's society. Following on from our guide to social media, let's look at online dating, and love in general, and the many rules you need to follow...

HI!

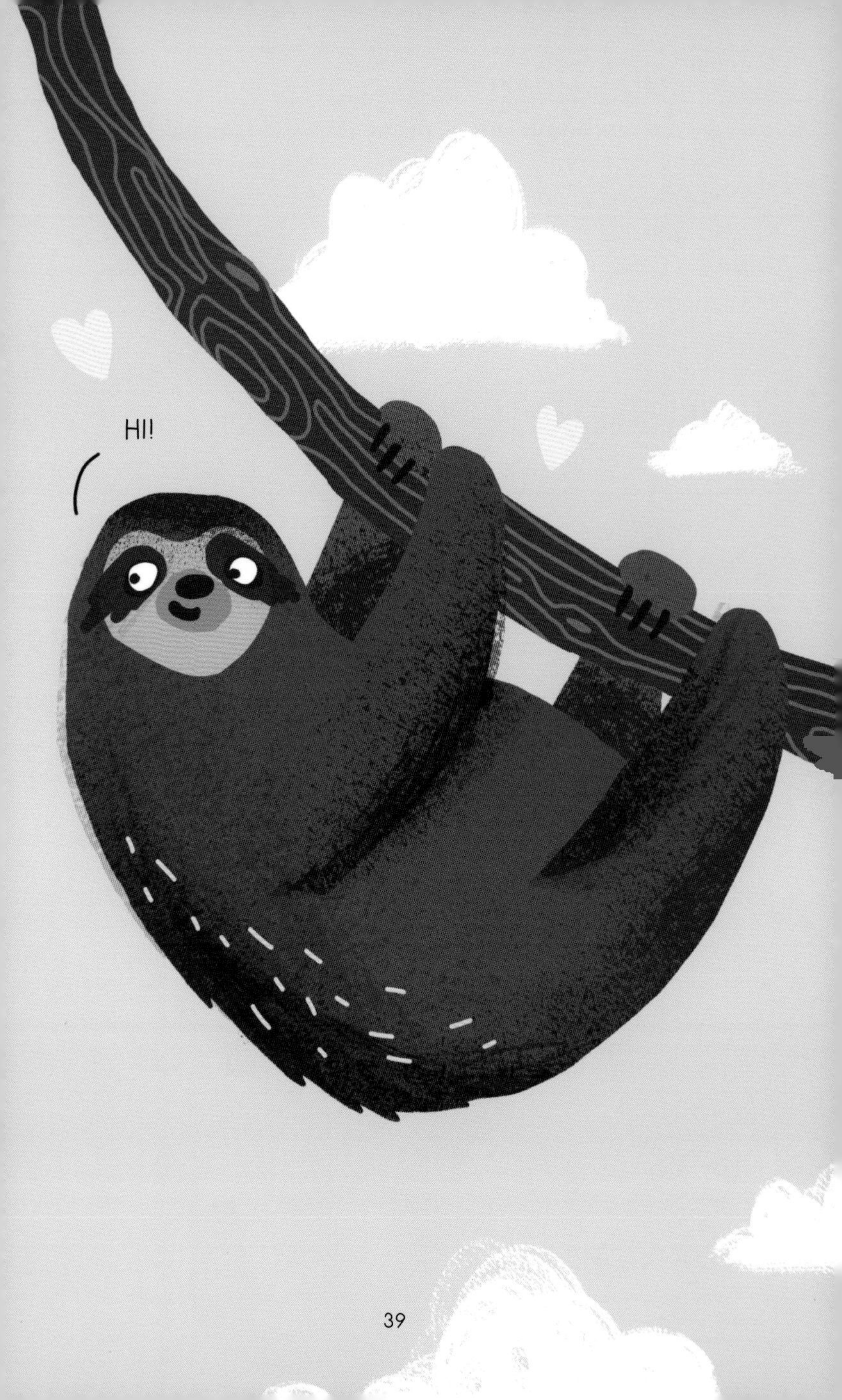
HI!

ONLINE DATING

The internet is a great place to meet people and to find a potential love interest, but some people's intentions aren't always genuine and you may end up getting in a pickle if you don't wise up to how it all works. Here are some scenarios that you should familiarize yourself with so you know what to look out for, and who to avoid...

GENERIC INTRODUCTIONS

Some people aren't too fussy when it comes to dating and will try their luck with as many people as they can get their hands on.

These people will not have taken the time to look at your profile and see what makes you tick. I can guarantee that the very same message will be hitting the inboxes of lots of other unlucky folk out there, too.

TOP TIP: look out for messages that seem overly generic or make references that don't seem to relate to you or your profile...

YOU HAVE PRETTY HAIR. WANT TO CHAT?

UNSOLICITED PICS

Don't be fooled by the simple eggplant/aubergine emoji. It's not a symbol for vegetable lovers, but a reference to a certain male body part that I'm too polite to mention! If anyone offers to send you pictures, politely decline.

BUT I JUST REALLY LIKE AUBERGINES?

CATFISHING

Catfishing is where internet predators make up an online profile designed to lure unsuspecting prey. It's a relatively new phenomenon, which has fooled many naive daters out there and is very bad etiquette.

My advice: watch out for those who tell you exactly what you want to hear. They're most likely fibbing.

THE ILLUSION

FRIENDLY MOUSE LOOKING FOR A RODENT COMPANION TO SHARE CHEESE FONDUE WITH. NOT FUSSY.

NB: catfishing does not exclusively apply to cats or fish. It can apply to anyone who pretends to be someone or something they are not.

COMMUNICATION

So you've met someone you like and you've got their number... GREAT! But now what?

Well, it's time to arrange a first date. You don't want to be too quick to do this or you risk sounding desperate, so leave it a day or two and then send a quick message asking if they fancy meeting up for a drink/dinner/romantic walk/joint nap. Then wait for the reply...

HOW LONG DO I WAIT?

Be patient my little worry worm. I know waiting for a response may feel like torture, but you need to give it time.

0 NEW TEXTS

OK. I'VE WAITED FIVE MINUTES. SHOULD I SEND ANOTHER?

Absolutely not. Never double text. It looks *waaay* too desperate.

BUT WHAT IF THEY NEVER REPLY?

Well, that's just too bad. But don't let it get you down... there are plenty more worms in the sea.

YOU'RE RIGHT. I DIDN'T EVEN LIKE HER THAT MUCH.

OH WAIT SHE'S JUST REPLIED!

FIRST DATE RULES

First dates are a great way to get to know someone and to find out if you like that person as much as you first thought. I'm a traditional kind of guy and like to make a lady feel special, so I never turn up to a date empty handed.

Don't be too flashy, however. Buying jewelry and extravagant gifts is not appropriate for a first date. I like to pick my own flowers for a personal, yet thrifty, gift.

COMPLIMENTS

Paying your date compliments will make them feel special and show that you're interested in them romantically. But make sure you don't go too overboard or it may make them uncomfortable...

MODERN WOMEN

Tip for guys: it's always been considered polite to open a door or hold back a low swinging branch for a lady. But know this: the modern-day woman doesn't want to be bound to old-fashioned values that see her as some poor damsel who needs rescuing. So, hold that door open for her, but make sure she coughs up for half the bill so that she knows you value her as an equal.

MAKE MINE A
DOUBLE, SUE.
AND THROW IN A
BAG OF PEANUTS.

PLAYING THE FIELD

This is the term used when someone is dating more than one person. It's a good way to keep your options open, but has the potential to upset a lot of people if they find out what you're up to. If you're going to be a "player" then it's best to be honest so people know the score from the offset.

GETTING SERIOUS

So things have gotten serious and you've decided to settle down... great news! If you've decided to move in together there are certain etiquettes that you should use around the house to make sure that you don't rub each other up the wrong way...

1. SHARE THE CHORES. It's important that neither of you feel like you're doing the lion's share of the housework (lions are notoriously tidy) while the other just lounges around all day getting their beauty sleep. Making a rota is a useful way of sharing the chores, ensuring that you're both pulling your weight and avoiding any resentment that may fester otherwise.

	ME	YOU
MONDAY	SLEEP	SLEEP
TUESDAY	GATHER GRUBS	SLEEP
WEDNESDAY	SLEEP	SLEEP
THURSDAY	SLEEP	TIDY BRANCH
FRIDAY	SLEEP	SLEEP
SATURDAY	SLEEP	SLEEP
SUNDAY	SLEEP	SLEEP

2. ALWAYS MAKE PLENTY OF TIME FOR CUDDLES. It's important that you let your loved one know how special they are, and what better way than by having a spoon. NB: make sure that you agree on your preferred spooning position early on so you know you're compatible.

MOVING ON

If you think a relationship has run it's course then it's time to let that person know it's over. Some say honesty is the best policy, but I prefer to go for something a little kinder...

IT'S NOT YOU, IT'S ME...

(... SHE'S JUST TOO CLINGY.)

IT'S NOT YOU, IT'S ME...

(... YOU ARE SUFFOCATING ME AND I CAN'T BREATHE. LITERALLY.)

GHOSTING

Ghosting is a modern phrase that describes the act of suddenly ignoring somebody after dating them, in the hope that they will just "get the message."

It's bad etiquette to ghost somebody. You should always let someone know when the relationship is over, rather than leave them hanging...

NB: if you are dating a sloth and are concerned that you are being ghosted, please remember that we do sometimes sleep for up to 24 hours at a time, so you should bear that in mind before worrying we've turned into a ghost.

GETTING DUMPED

Not all relationshps are meant to be, but being dumped is never fun. As a general rule, if the person has let you down gently, with compassion and kindness, then the right thing to do is to hold your head up high and move on with dignity.

Try spending time with friends, who will often have some wise words to help cheer you up.

If you were treated badly (ghosted, cheated on, lied to, etc...), then I think it's perfectly acceptable to serve them up some just desserts...

SHHH...

IT'S TIME FOR A RECAP

We're nearly at the end of our journey to pitch perfect etiquette, so let's have a quick recap...

We've learnt the basic rules of etiquette, how to behave at weddings, dinner parties, and in the workplace. Plus we've delved into the dos and don'ts of dating, dumping, and socializing on the world wide web. PHEW! I need a nap after all that.

I hope you're finding these tips as useful as Tony is... just look how far he's come.

I LIKE YOUR LITTLE HAT TONY.

(I'M NOT REALLY SURE WHY TONY IS WEARING A TOP HAT, BUT IT DOES LOOK SMART.)

We've got one more subject to cover and it's the most difficult of them all... STICKY SITUATIONS!

And by "sticky situation" I don't mean being on the recieving end of an anteater's kiss (although that is a very sticky situation indeed).

No, no. I'm referring to those awkward situations that you may find yourself in from time to time, which require some special etiquette to get you through in one piece. Let's look at a couple of awkward instances and how to deal with them...

1. FORGETTING SOMEONE'S NAME. Oh this is terribly embarrassing, but sometimes it's difficult to remember the name of EVERYBODY you've met. You could ask them to remind you of their name, but that will show them that they were too boring to be remembered the first time round. Instead, try throwing in the odd term of endearment and they'll be none the wiser.

2. FORGETTING SOMEONE'S BIRTHDAY. This isn't good and you need to think fast in order to stop the potential catastrophe that you've caused. You have a number of options:

a. Blame the postal service and hope you can get something to arrive promptly the next day.

b. Confess and run the risk of them reminding you of your negligence every year for the rest of time.

c. Get creative. Make something extra special with some materials that you have close to hand. This one-of-a-kind gift will mean even more to them than something you've just ordered off the internet.

3. PARPING IN PUBLIC. It's not good etiquette to pass wind (or trump/toot/bottom burp/fluff/fart/cut the cheese, etc.) around others, but sometimes these things happen (especially with a diet so high in fiber).

So, you're with company and you've let the cat out of the bag (so to speak), and it's obvious that someone's to blame...

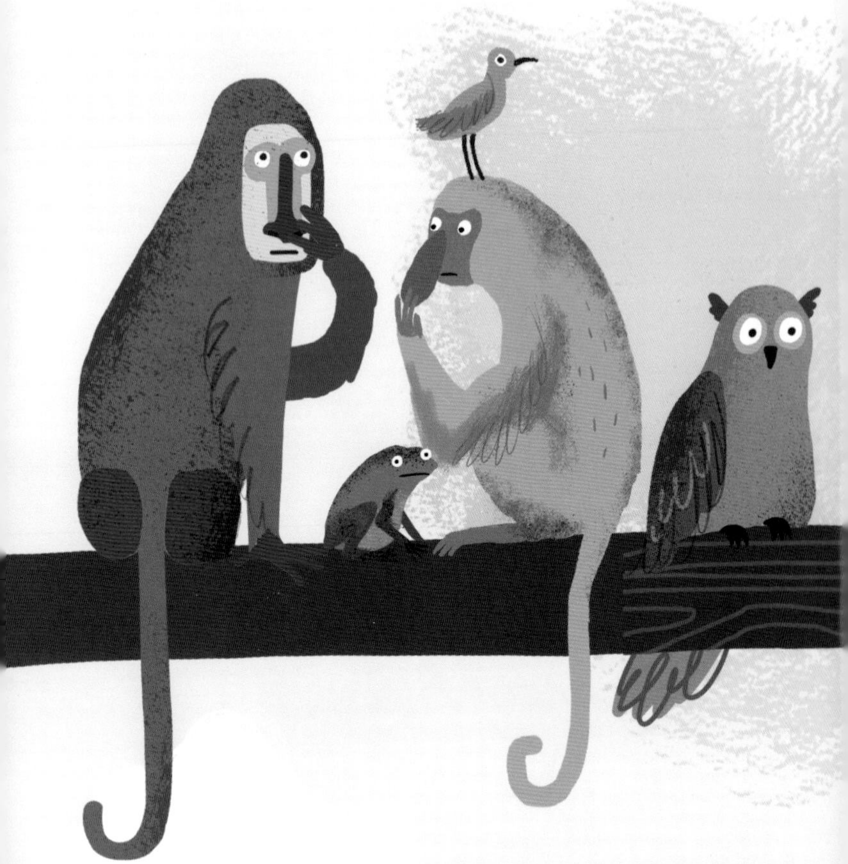

Here's the number one rule... don't admit to anything.

If you do, you'll forever be known as farty pants and that's a hard label to shake off.

Just act casual, don't point the finger of blame at anyone else, and act like it never happened. Then hope for a gust of wind to clear the air.

AND FINALLY...

Here's my last bit of advice on how to behave properly and my number one tip for good etiquette. If you forget everything else I've taught you throughout this book, then please try to remember this very important bit of advice, which will help you breeze through whatever situation comes your way with the utmost class and decorum...

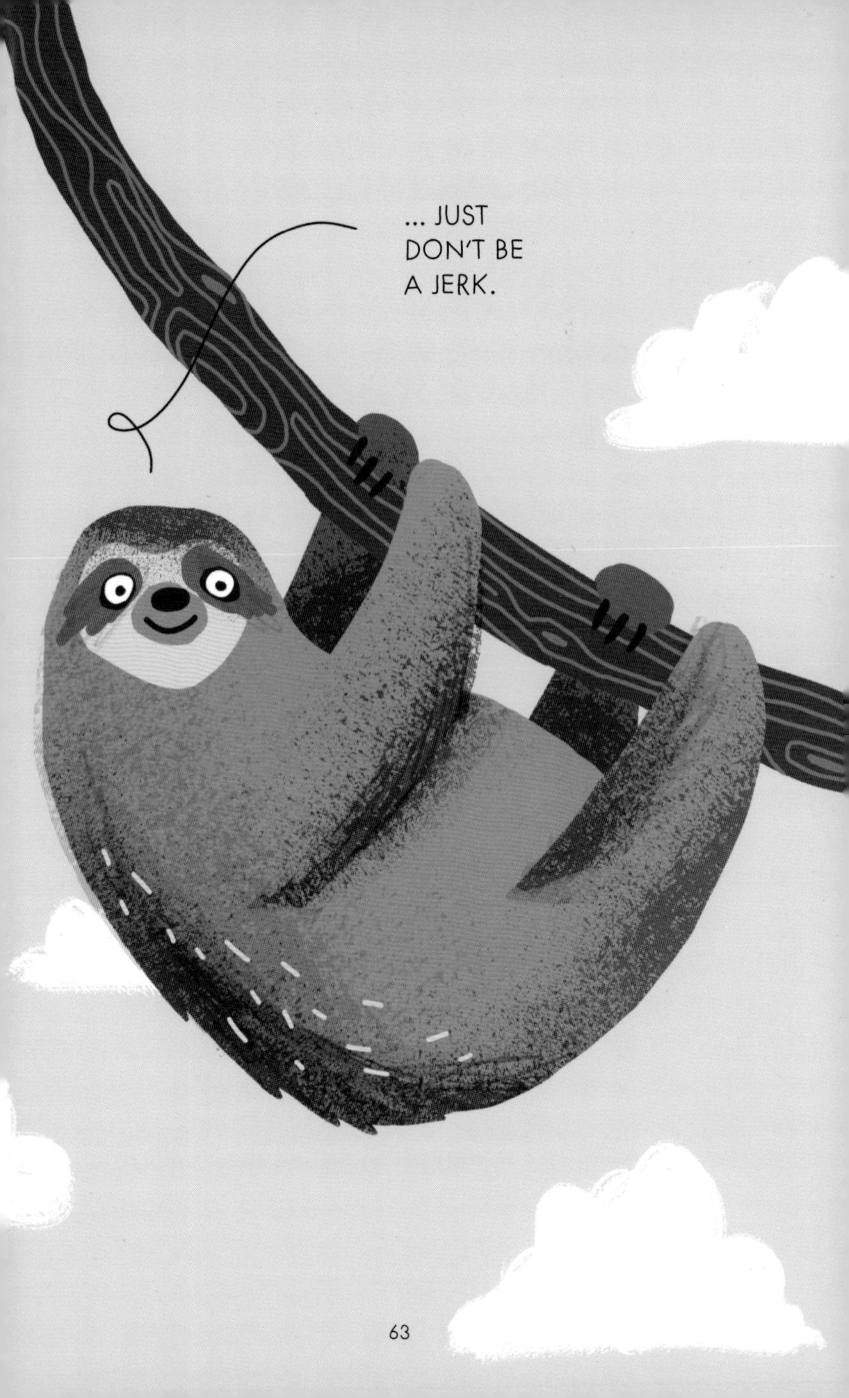
... JUST
DON'T BE
A JERK.

ACKNOWLEDGMENTS

I'd like to dedicate this book to my mum and dad, who taught me all of the manners that I manage to possess today. I think they did a pretty good job, but I may be biased...